THIS
BELO

G00010819

Name: Age:

Favourite player:

2022/2023

My Predictions...   **Actual...**

The Hornets' final position:

The Hornets' top scorer:

Sky Bet Championship winners:

Sky Bet Championship top scorer:

FA Cup winners:

EFL Cup winners:

Contributors: Tom Baldwin, Elliot Murray, Peter Rogers and Peter White.

A TWOCAN PUBLICATION

©2022. Published by twocan under licence from Watford Football Club.

ISBN: 978-1-914588-69-3

PICTURE CREDITS:
Action Images, Alamy, Alan Cozzi and Press Association.

£9

CONTENTS

GOAL OF THE SEASON

CUCHO HERNÁNDEZ

Colombian attacker Cucho Hernández won Watford FC's 2021/22 Goal of the Season award for his bicycle-kick strike against Arsenal in March 2022.

Signed in 2017, Hernández spent most of his Watford career out on loan in his native Colombia and the top two Spanish divisions. Earning promotion with Huesca to La Liga and later joining RCD Mallorca and Getafe on temporary deals, the forward notably scored against Real Madrid and Barcelona in the top tier before joining up with his parent club.

Hernández, who netted five times in total during the Premier League campaign before departing for MLS side Columbus Crew in June 2022, found the target with an acrobatic strike against the Gunners at Vicarage Road.

Minutes after Martin Ødegaard's opener looked to have shell-shocked the hosts, Hernández produced a moment of magic to bring the two sides on level terms.

Emmanuel Dennis laid the ball off to Kiko Femenía on the right flank, with the Spaniard delivering a lofted, out-swinging cross into the path of teammate Hernández. The acrobatic forward connected with the pass mid-flight to find the bottom corner, beating goalkeeper Aaron Ramsdale.

The crowd at The Vic jumped to their feet in astonishment, with their mouths agog at the superb effort. Not many had seen a bicycle kick nestle quite so sweetly into the back of the net.

Despite the match ending in a 3-2 defeat to Arsenal, with Moussa Sissoko the other goalscorer for the Hornets, the game will always be remembered for the athletic offering from Hernández, a stand-out moment in the season.

THE NOMINEES...

CUCHO HERNÁNDEZ V ASTON VILLA

Hernández's spectacular opening-day goal against the Villans less than a minute after his introduction from the bench was also a contender for the award.

Cutting inside from the edge of the box, his shot looped impressively into the top corner sending the Watford faithful into raptures.

EMMANUEL DENNIS V WEST HAM UNITED

Watford's top marksman scored an impressive array of goals in the 2021/22 campaign, but his strike against West Ham United in late December may have been the most skilful.

Patiently waiting to shoot, Dennis' dummy saw Craig Dawson slide to the floor, providing the space to unleash a rocket which flew into the roof of the net.

NUMBER OF SEASONS
WITH THE HORNETS:

9

WATFORD
LEAGUE APPEARANCES:

234

WATFORD LEAGUE GOALS:

42

LEGEND

NIGEL CALLAGHAN

WATFORD ACHIEVEMENTS:

Division Two runners-up 1981/82
Division One runners-up 1982/83
FA Cup runners-up 1983/84

MAJOR STRENGTH:

An outstanding crosser of the ball
who was able to pick out a teammate
with pin-point accuracy

INTERNATIONAL ACTION:

Nigel was capped by England at both
U21 and B level as a Watford player

FINEST HOUR:

Scoring nine top-flight goals as Watford
took the First Division by storm in 1981/82

Top quality wingers Nigel Callaghan and Gerard Deulofeu were two of the most exciting wide-men to pull on the famous yellow Watford shirt and both made a big impression during their respective careers at Vicarage Road.

Callaghan and Deulofeu were clear match-winners on their day and blessed with the skill and talent to turn games in the Hornets' favour. With the ability to score goals and create chances for teammates, these two former Watford stars were both real crowd favourites at the Vic. Each player has a Watford FA Cup final appearance on their CV - but who was the best? That's for you to decide and here are a few facts and figures from their time in Watford colours to help you reach your conclusion...

It's a tough call...!

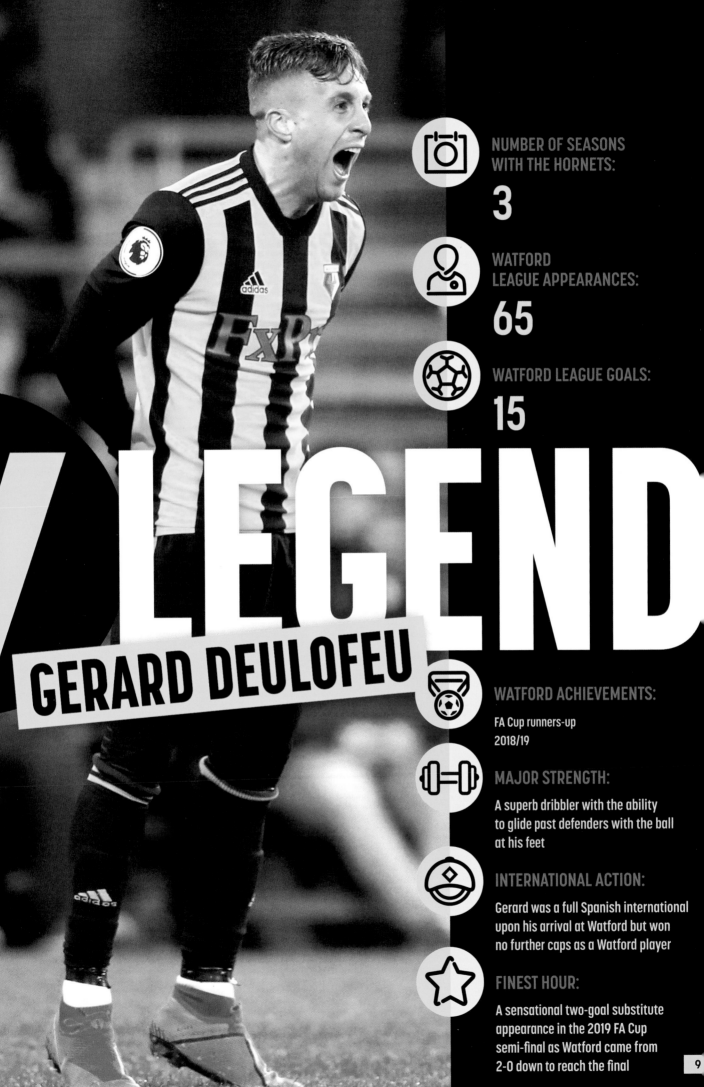

LEGEND

GERARD DEULOFEU

NUMBER OF SEASONS WITH THE HORNETS:

3

WATFORD LEAGUE APPEARANCES:

65

WATFORD LEAGUE GOALS:

15

WATFORD ACHIEVEMENTS:

FA Cup runners-up 2018/19

MAJOR STRENGTH:

A superb dribbler with the ability to glide past defenders with the ball at his feet

INTERNATIONAL ACTION:

Gerard was a full Spanish international upon his arrival at Watford but won no further caps as a Watford player

FINEST HOUR:

A sensational two-goal substitute appearance in the 2019 FA Cup semi-final as Watford came from 2-0 down to reach the final

EDO
KAYEMBE
39

Defending is not just about stopping the attackers and clearing your lines. Making the best of possession you have just won is vital - although the danger has to be cleared, it is important for your team to keep hold of the ball.

SOCCER SKILLS
LONG PASSES

When passing your way out of defence, and short, side-foot passes are not possible, the longer pass, driven over the heads of midfield players, can be used.

EXERCISE

In an area 40m x 10m, A1 and A2 try to pass accurately to each other, with a defender B, in the middle between them. Player B must attempt to stop the pass if possible, and A1 and A2, must keep the ball within the area of the grids.

After each successful long pass, the end player will exchange a shorter pass with B before passing long again, thus keeping the exercise realistic and also keeping the defender in the middle involved. The player in the middle should be changed every few minutes, and a 'count' of successful passes made for each player.

KEY FACTORS

1. Approach at an angle.
2. Non kicking foot placed next to the ball.
3. Eye on the ball.
4. Strike underneath the ball & follow through.

Practice is the key to striking a consistently accurate long pass and to developing the timing and power required.

The same end result could be achieved by bending the pass around the defender instead of over him, and this pass could be practised in the same exercise, by striking the football on its outer edge (instead of underneath) which will impart the spin required to make the ball 'bend' around the defender - not an easy skill!

WATFORD

CHAMPIONSHIP
2022/2023
SQUAD

1 DANIEL BACHMANN
GOALKEEPER DOB: 09/07/1994 COUNTRY: AUSTRIA

A Watford shot-stopper since 2017 and now a full Austria international, 28-year-old Daniel Bachmann occupied the sticks in half of the Hornets games as they were promoted from the Championship in 2020/21, making a further 12 appearances in the Premier League last season. Bachmann was Austria's main goalkeeper at Euro 2020 as his nation reached the Round of 16.

2 JEREMY NGAKIA
DEFENDER DOB: 07/09/2000 COUNTRY: ENGLAND

Signed from West Ham United in 2020, young right-back Jeremy Ngakia has impressed Watford fans with his committed performances in defence in the Championship and Premier League. Ngakia made his top-flight debut for the Hammers as a teenager against Liverpool and put in an assured performance against the-then European champions, before swapping East London for Hertfordshire that summer to play regular first-team football.

3 MARIO GASPAR

DEFENDER   DOB: 24/11/1990   COUNTRY: **SPAIN**

Defender Mario Gaspar joined the Hornets in July 2022, following his departure from La Liga side Villarreal.

The Spaniard arrived in Hertfordshire after plying his trade at the Estadio de la Cerámica for over a decade, having risen through the Yellow Submarine's youth and reserve ranks to make his first-team debut in March 2009, and gone on to serve as club captain.

4 HAMZA CHOUDHURY

MIDFIELDER   DOB: 01/10/1997   COUNTRY: ENGLAND

Highly-rated midfielder Hamza Choudhury joined the Hornets in August 2022 on a season-long loan with an option to buy.

The 25-year-old moved from Premier League side Leicester City, where he plied his trade from the age of seven and made a total of 84 first-team appearances since his debut against Liverpool in the Carabao Cup in September 2017. An England youth international, Choudhury has amassed seven caps for the Under-21s having made his debut against China in May 2018, while he also represented the Young Lions at the 2019 UEFA U21 European Championships in Italy.

5 WILLIAM TROOST-EKONG

DEFENDER DOB: 01/09/1993 COUNTRY: NIGERIA

The son-in-law of a Watford supporter and Season Ticket holder, defender William Troost-Ekong was well aware of the Hornets when he signed from Udinese in 2020. The Dutch-born Nigeria international, who captains his national side, was key to the Golden Boys' solidity in defence in his first campaign at the club, playing 17 times in the Premier League one season later.

6 IMRÂN LOUZA

MIDFIELDER DOB: 01/05/1999 COUNTRY: MOROCCO

Creative midfielder Imrân Louza had spent his whole life in Nantes before Watford came calling in the summer of 2021. The Morocco international, born in the French town, came through the ranks at the team nicknamed 'The Yellow House' and played his first senior game in 2019. Louza played 20 league games in his first season in England, establishing himself in the Watford side at the base of midfield.

7 KEINAN DAVIS

FORWARD   DOB: **13/02/1998**   COUNTRY: **ENGLAND**

Keinan Davis joined Watford on loan from Aston Villa in August 2022. The talented striker signed after successfully helping Nottingham Forest to Premier League promotion during a loan spell earlier in 2022.

At the City Ground, Davis played a key role in Forest's promotion campaign, scoring five goals in 14 matches, featuring in the Play-Off semi-finals against Sheffield United and the final victory over Huddersfield Town.

8 TOM CLEVERLEY

MIDFIELDER   DOB: **12/08/1989**   COUNTRY: **ENGLAND**

Club captain Tom Cleverley has won promotion, scored crucial winning goals and reached an FA Cup final in his two spells as a Hornet, and is now seeking to return to the Premier League in a Watford shirt once again. Joining initially on loan from Manchester United and winning Player of the Season in 2009/10, the England international returned to Hertfordshire in 2017 and has turned out for the Golden Boys ever since.

9 REY MANAJ

FORWARD DOB: 24/02/1997 COUNTRY: ALBANIA

Albanian striker Rey Manaj swapped FC Barcelona for Watford in the lead up to the 2022/23 Sky Bet Championship season, becoming the first player to inherit club legend Troy Deeney's number nine shirt. The 25-year-old made his debut coming off the bench in a memorable 1-0 win over Sheffield United, and he provides physicality and drive to the Golden Boys' attack.

10 JOÃO PEDRO

FORWARD DOB: 26/09/2001 COUNTRY: BRAZIL

Hoping to improve on the nine goals he notched in his first season in the Sky Bet Championship, versatile Brazilian attacker João Pedro scored his first goal in the second tier on his 19th birthday, becoming the first player in 14 years to net the winner in a derby fixture against Luton Town in 2020. Since then he has scored an emotional first top-flight strike against Manchester United and led the line in style for Watford, netting against the likes of Newcastle United and Leicester City last season.

CHAMPIONSHIP
2022/2023
SQUAD

12 KEN SEMA

MIDFIELDER **DOB:** 30/09/1993 **COUNTRY:** SWEDEN

An energetic dribbler capable of playing on the left of attack or at wing-back, Swedish wide man Ken Sema has been a Watford player since 2018. Sema spent a season on loan at Italian club Udinese in his second year at Vicarage Road, and has racked up over a dozen international caps so far in his career.

14 HASSANE KAMARA

DEFENDER **DOB:** 05/03/1994 **COUNTRY:** IVORY COAST

Attacking full-back Hassane Kamara has graced the left and right side of defence since joining Watford in January 2022, entertaining supporters on and off the pitch with passionate displays and ventures into the crowd at full-time. Kamara found the target in a Watford shirt for the first time against Manchester City in April 2022, and made 19 appearances that season, missing a single game through suspension.

15 CRAIG CATHCART

DEFENDER **DOB:** 06/02/1989 **COUNTRY:** N. IRELAND

Club stalwart Craig Cathcart is the current longest-serving player at the club, joining in the season of Watford's promotion to the Premier League in 2014/15. Cathcart had spent time at Vicarage Road on loan in 2009 also, and has since become a vital player during some of the Hornets' most successful years. The Northern Irishman has played over 100 top-flight games for the Golden Boys, won two promotions and reached an FA Cup final.

16 DAN GOSLING

MIDFIELDER **DOB:** 01/02/1990 **COUNTRY:** ENGLAND

Boasting years of pedigree in the Championship and Premier League, Dan Gosling swapped AFC Bournemouth for Watford in January 2020, scoring a vital goal against Norwich as the Hornets pipped the Cherries to promotion that year. Gosling, 32, has also played for the likes of Newcastle and Everton in his career, and scored a powerful header in the Golden Boys' most recent top-flight game against Chelsea.

CHAMPIONSHIP
2022/2023
SQUAD

18 YÁSER ASPRILLA

MIDFIELDER   DOB: 19/11/2003   COUNTRY: COLOMBIA

Arriving a fresh faced 18-year-old in 2022/23 pre-season, Colombian playmaker Yáser Asprilla didn't appear affected by the language barrier as he showed off talent and composure in warm-up games, even netting against Wycombe Wanderers. Asprilla joined the Hornets from Envigado in his native country, where he caught the eye of the national team, making his debut in January 2022.

19 VAKOUN BAYO

FORWARD   DOB: 10/01/1997   COUNTRY: IVORY COAST

Dangerous in the air and an accomplished finisher in several countries, Vakoun Bayo started a new challenge with Watford in July 2022, having already played in Belgium, France and other footballing nations. The Ivorian, whose hero is Chelsea legend Didier Drogba, attracted widespread attention for his goalscoring form at the back end of the 2021/22 campaign with Belgian side Charleroi.

19

23 ISMAÏLA SARR

FORWARD DOB: 25/02/1998 COUNTRY: SENEGAL

Watford's record signing Ismaïla Sarr became a Hornet in August 2020, signing from French outfit Rennes. The speedster, who finished club top goalscorer in the 2020/21 campaign and scored two memorable goals in the defeat of Liverpool the season prior, typically operates from the right flank but has also played as a striker on occasion at Vicarage Road.

24 TOM DELE-BASHIRU

MIDFIELDER DOB: 17/09/1999 COUNTRY: NIGERIA

Recovering from a serious knee injury and spending the 2021/22 season on loan at Reading, Manchester City youth product Tom Dele-Bashiru is no stranger to the second tier, amassing 25 league appearances last term. Dele-Bashiru's first goal for the Hornets came in a 2020 FA Cup fixture against Tranmere Rovers, with the Nigerian slamming home from outside the box.

26 BEN HAMER

GOALKEEPER DOB: 20/11/1987 COUNTRY: ENGLAND

Inheriting the number 26 shirt previously worn by Daniel Bachmann and Ben Foster, accomplished glovesman Ben Hamer added more Championship experience to the goalkeeping department when he arrived on a free transfer in July 2022. Hamer has played for the likes of Swansea City, Huddersfield Town and Leicester City over the years, playing a UEFA Champions League match for the latter.

27 CHRISTIAN KABASELE

DEFENDER DOB: 24/02/1991 COUNTRY: BELGIUM

Belgian centre-half Christian Kabasele arrived at Watford off the back of a highly successful campaign with Genk, winning the club's Player of the Season award in 2015/16. A firm favourite among Watford supporters for his commitment on the pitch and charisma off it, the 31-year-old has played over 100 Premier League games in yellow. A striker in his early career, a young Kabasele became a central defender on loan at KAS Eupen, adapting to the role and impressing coaches in his native country, continuing in the position to this day.

30 KORTNEY HAUSE

DEFENDER   DOB: 16/07/1995   COUNTRY: ENGLAND

Kortney Hause signed for the Hornets on a season-long loan from Aston Villa in August 2022. The ex-Wycombe and Wolves defender arrived with a wealth of experience at all levels of the Football League pyramid - including a previous promotion to the top-flight with the Villans. Hause was part of the England Under-21 side that won the Toulon Tournament in 2016.

28 SAMUEL KALU

FORWARD   DOB: 26/08/1997   COUNTRY: NIGERIA

Following spells at sides in Slovakia, Belgium and France, Samuel Kalu started a new challenge at Watford in January 2022, joining from Girondins de Bordeaux. The Nigeria international can play on either flank or as a striker, and made his Vicarage Road debut against Arsenal in March. Kalu has amassed over 15 international caps too, notching his first goal for the Super Eagles against Libya in October 2018.

31 FRANCISCO SIERRALTA

DEFENDER   DOB: 06/05/1997   COUNTRY: CHILE

A mainstay in the 2020/21 Championship defence that conceded just 30 goals all season, Chilean international defender Francisco Sierralta arrived from Udinese at the start of that campaign a relative unknown among Watford supporters but made an excellent impression when he became a regular in the side. The former Parma and Empoli centre-half moved to Europe in 2017 from the capital of his home country, Santiago, where he plied his trade with Universidad Católica.

32 MATTIE POLLOCK

DEFENDER   DOB: 28/09/2001   COUNTRY: ENGLAND

Young centre-half Mattie Pollock's performances for League Two Grimsby Town resulted in his Watford move in the summer of 2021. Then a teenager, Pollock had made 58 appearances for the Mariners and was ready for a step up, and this was proven in his successful loan spell at League One side Cheltenham Town in the 2021/22 campaign, playing 39 games and picking up the Young Player of the Season award for the Robins.

35 MADUKA OKOYE

GOALKEEPER   DOB: 28/08/1999   COUNTRY: NIGERIA

Nigeria number one Maduka Okoye's final season at Sparta Rotterdam before moving to Watford ended in jubilation, as his old side escaped almost-certain relegation in the final weeks of the Eredivisie campaign. Okoye agreed terms with the Hornets halfway through the 2021/22 season but remained on loan at his former club, and earned a spot in the Super Eagles' Africa Cup of Nations squad for his consistent displays in goal.

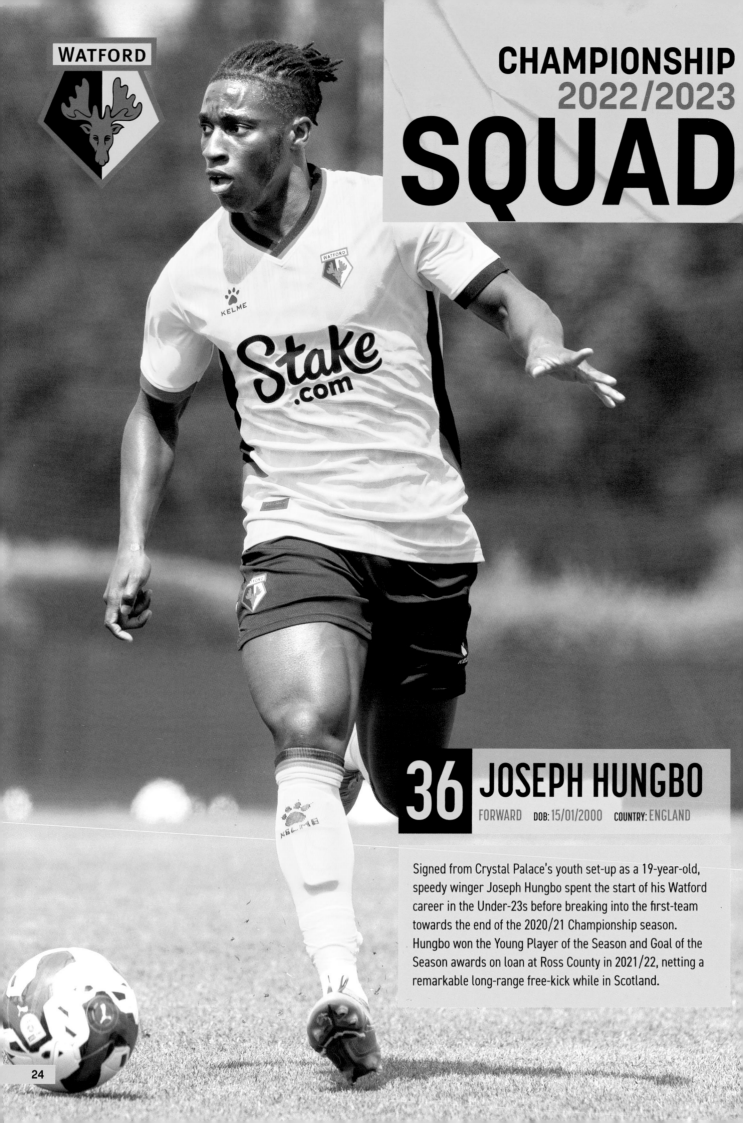

WATFORD

36 JOSEPH HUNGBO

FORWARD   DOB: 15/01/2000   COUNTRY: ENGLAND

Signed from Crystal Palace's youth set-up as a 19-year-old, speedy winger Joseph Hungbo spent the start of his Watford career in the Under-23s before breaking into the first-team towards the end of the 2020/21 Championship season. Hungbo won the Young Player of the Season and Goal of the Season awards on loan at Ross County in 2021/22, netting a remarkable long-range free-kick while in Scotland.

39 EDO KAYEMBE

MIDFIELDER   DOB: **03/06/1998**   COUNTRY: **DR CONGO**

Left-footed midfielder Edo Kayembe became a Hornet in January 2022 following a successful spell at KAS Eupen in Belgium. Kayembe had previously played for Anderlecht in the same country, and was effective in a defensive role and further forward. The DR Congo international has experience playing European football, and featured 13 times for Watford in 2021/22.

41 VINCENT ANGELINI

GOALKEEPER   DOB: **12/09/2003**   COUNTRY: SCOTLAND

Scottish-Italian goalkeeper Vincent Angelini arrived in Hertfordshire in 2021 as a highly-rated prospect between the sticks. The former Celtic glovesman regularly features for the Hornets' Under-21 side, and he made the first-team bench on three occasions during the 2021/22 Premier League campaign.

WATFORD

MULTIPLE CHOICE

Here are ten Multiple Choice questions to challenge your footy knowledge!

Good luck...

ANSWERS ON PAGE 62

1. What was the name of Tottenham Hotspur's former ground?

A) White Rose Park
B) White Foot Way
C) White Hart Lane

2. Which club did Steven Gerrard leave to become Aston Villa manager?

A) Liverpool
B) Glasgow Rangers
C) LA Galaxy

3. Mohamed Salah and Son Heung-min were joint winners of the Premier League Golden Boot as the division's top scorers in 2021/22.

How many goals did they score?

A) 23   B) 24   C) 25

4. What is the nationality of Manchester United boss Erik ten Hag?

A) Swiss   B) Dutch
C) Swedish

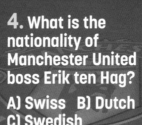

5. Where do Everton play their home games?

A) Goodison Road
B) Goodison Way
C) Goodison Park

6. From which club did Arsenal sign goalkeeper Aaron Ramsdale?

A) Sheffield United
B) Stoke City
C) AFC Bournemouth

7. What is Raheem Sterling's middle name?

A) Shaun
B) Shaquille
C) Silver

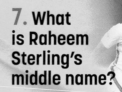

8. Who won the 2021/22 League One Play-Off final?

A) Wigan Athletic
B) Sunderland
C) Rotherham United

9. How many times have Watford reached the FA Cup final?

A) Once
B) Twice
C) Three times

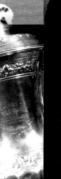

10. Which club did Rob Edwards guide to the League Two title in 2021/22?

A) Bristol Rovers
B) Port Vale
C) Forest Green Rovers

26

TOM
CLEVERLEY

8

ANSWERS ON PAGE 62

CLASSIC FAN'TASTIC

Harry the Hornet is hiding in the crowd in five different places as Watford fans celebrate promotion to the Premier League in 2015. Can you find all five?

DANIEL
BACHMANN

Close control in tight situations creates havoc in opposition defences - particularly when receiving the ball in the air - and nine times out of ten, when a striker receives the ball, he has his back to goal.

SOCCER SKILLS
RECEIVING THE BALL

Quite often the ball will arrive in the air, and good strikers have to be able to cope with that - controlling and turning in one movement, ready for the instant shot.

EXERCISE 1

In an area 20m x 10m, two players A and A2 test the man in the middle, B, by initially throwing the ball at him in the air, with the instruction to turn and play in to the end man - if possible using only two touches.

The middle player is changed regularly, and to make things more realistic, the end players progress to chipping the ball into the middle.

The middle player is asked to receive and turn using chest, thigh, or instep.

KEY FACTORS

1 Assess flight early - get in position.
2 Cushion the ball.
3 Be half turned as you receive.

EXERCISE 2

A progression of this exercise is the following, where the ball is chipped or driven in to the striker from varying positions. He has to receive with his back to goal, and using just two touches in total if possible, shoot past the keeper into the goal!

To make this even more difficult, a defender can be brought in eventually. For younger children, the 'servers' should throw the ball to ensure consistent quality.

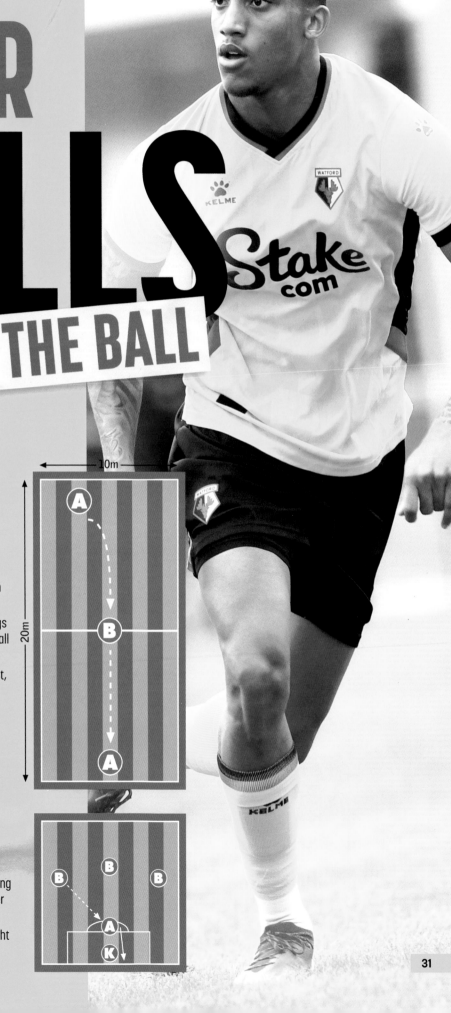

TRAIN TO WIN

Making sure that you are fit, healthy and fully prepared is key to success in whatever challenge you are taking on. Those three factors are certainly vital for professional footballers and also for any young aspiring player who plays for his or her school or local football team. The importance of fitness, health and preparation are key factors behind the work that goes into preparing the Watford players to perform at their maximum on matchday.

The Hornets players will need to demonstrate peak levels of fitness if they want to feature in Rob Edwards' team. Before anyone can think of pulling on a smart yellow shirt and stepping out at Vicarage Road, they will have had to perform well at the Training Ground to have shown the manager, his coaches and fitness staff that they are fully fit and ready for the physical challenges that await them on a matchday.

Regardless of whether training takes place at the training ground or at the stadium, the players' fitness remains an all-important factor. Of course time spent practicing training drills and playing small-sided games will help a player's fitness but there is lots of work undertaken just to ensure maximum levels of fitness are reached.

Away from the training pitches the players will spend a great deal of time in the gymnasium partaking in their own personal work-outs. Bikes, treadmills and weights will all form part of helping the players reach and maintain a top level of fitness.

Over the course of a week the players will take part in many warm-up and aerobic sessions and even complete yoga and pilates classes to help with core strength and general fitness. The strength and conditioning coaches at the club work tirelessly to do all they can to make sure that the players you see in action are at their physical peak come kick-off.

While the manager and his staff will select the team and agree the tactics, analysts will provide the players and staff with details on the opposition's strengths, weaknesses and their likely approach to the match.

Suffice to say the training ground is a busy place and no stone is left unturned in preparation for the big match!

PLAYER OF THE YEAR

HASSANE KAMARA

Full-back Hassane Kamara was named 2021/22 Graham Taylor Player of the Season following a vote by supporters at the end of the last campaign.

The Ivorian defender made an instant impact after signing from French side OGC Nice in January 2022, with his committed performances from left-back proving a hit with the Watford faithful at home and on the road.

Kamara made his debut against Newcastle United alongside fellow newcomers Samir and Edo Kayembe, putting in an effective display in a 1-1 draw at St James' Park. He became part of a defence that kept three clean sheets in six games in February under Roy Hodgson.

Quickly settling in, Kamara made more interceptions than any other Watford player despite his later arrival, displaying a tireless, high-octane style of play on the left side. The flying full-back missed just one game in the Premier League in the season of his arrival, starting in all but one of those matches.

His excellent start to life as a Hornet earned a recall to the Ivory Coast squad, with Kamara playing against England at Wembley in March.

He scored his first goal in a Watford shirt against Manchester City in April, making a tearing run through the City defence, receiving possession and driving a powerful low strike past Ederson.

Kamara came out on top of an online vote for the award, with Ben Foster runner-up and Emmanuel Dennis in third.

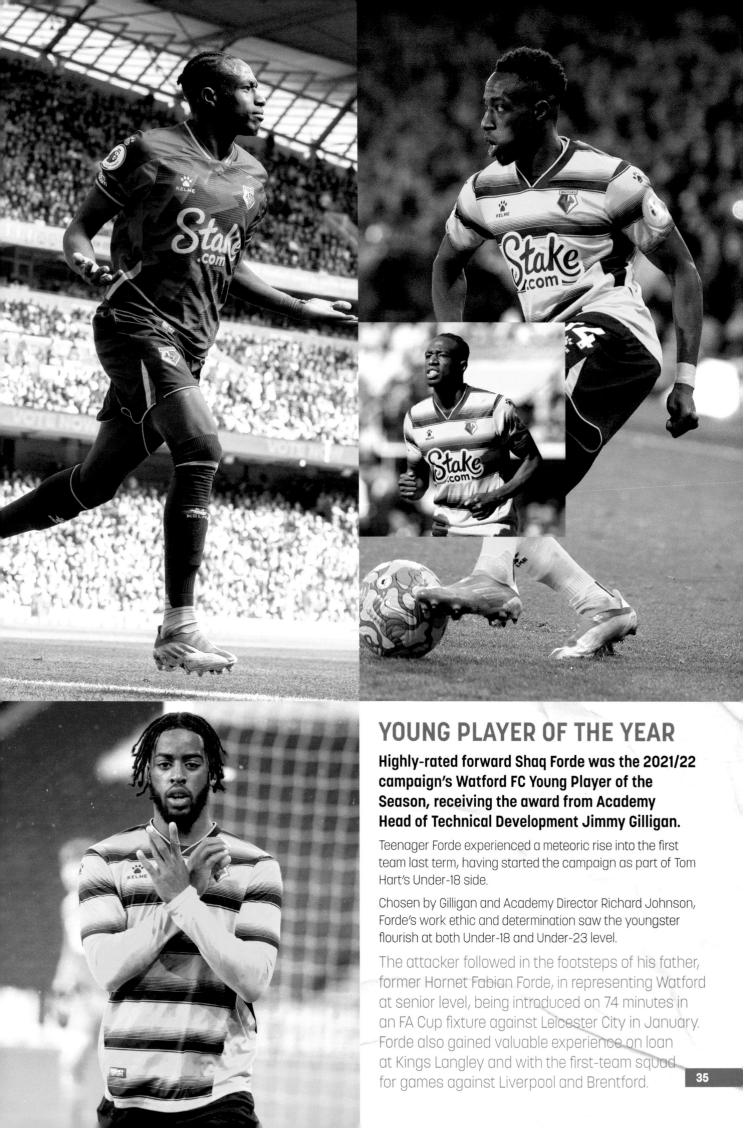

YOUNG PLAYER OF THE YEAR

Highly-rated forward Shaq Forde was the 2021/22 campaign's Watford FC Young Player of the Season, receiving the award from Academy Head of Technical Development Jimmy Gilligan.

Teenager Forde experienced a meteoric rise into the first team last term, having started the campaign as part of Tom Hart's Under-18 side.

Chosen by Gilligan and Academy Director Richard Johnson, Forde's work ethic and determination saw the youngster flourish at both Under-18 and Under-23 level.

The attacker followed in the footsteps of his father, former Hornet Fabian Forde, in representing Watford at senior level, being introduced on 74 minutes in an FA Cup fixture against Leicester City in January. Forde also gained valuable experience on loan at Kings Langley and with the first-team squad for games against Liverpool and Brentford.

VICARAGE ROAD
CENTENARY

Supporters, players and members of the Watford community alike gathered to celebrate the centenary anniversary of Vicarage Road on Tuesday 30 August 2022.

The Hornets' first match at The Vic came in 1922 against Millwall and exactly 100 years later they faced Middlesbrough in the Sky Bet Championship.

A hugely special occasion featured plenty of memorable moments on the pitch and off it. Pre-match, the hallowed Vicarage Road turf welcomed home legends Lloyd Doyley and Adrian Mariappa, with the latter speaking to the Watford faithful for the first time since his departure, while Golden Boys favourite Nigel Gibbs made an appearance on the big screen having recorded a message for the supporters earlier in the day.

With the atmosphere at fever pitch, a pyrotechnics display followed to the tune of 'I'm Still Standing' by Honorary Life-President Elton John. The players were cloaked in the new black and white third shirt, a call back to the Watford kit from 1922.

After a breathtaking first-half, more former players and Watford icons from over the years took to the pitch to say a few words and greet the crowd, alongside the Vicarage Road 100 team of supporters and staff that put the special night together. Among the former players were Stewart Scullion, John Fairbrother and Peter Walker.

On the night, Walker, who played for the club in the early 1960s alongside legendary striker Cliff Holton, said: "It's my pleasure to be back. Cliff was an exceptional player and was way above Third Division standards – he was a First Division player. He was magnificent."

Representing the current crop of Hornets players, club captain Tom Cleverley put his emotions into words: "It's been brilliant to see all these former players. It's something the club does very well and we have honoured them this evening in a very classy way.

"Vicarage Road is a stadium that has played a big part in my career. Not only have some of the best parts of my footballing career taken place here, but some of the best parts of my life have taken place here."

After a special reunion, Watford crowned the night with a last-minute Vakoun Bayo winner to secure an important 2-1 win on an emotional and dramatic evening.

BIRMINGHAM CITY
PRZEMYSLAW PLACHETA

A Polish international and true speed merchant, Przemyslaw Placheta is on a season long loan at St Andrew's from Championship rivals Norwich City.

The 24-year-old forward tends to operate on the left side of the Blues' attack and marked his home debut for Birmingham City with a goal in their 2-1 victory over Huddersfield Town in August.

CHAMPIONSHIP
DANGER MEN

24 STARS TO WATCH OUT FOR DURING 2022/23

BRISTOL CITY
ANDREAS WEIMANN

Austrian international forward Andreas Weimann was the Robins' leading scorer last season with 22 goals in 45 Championship games.

An experienced and proven goalscorer at this level, Weimann, who had scored goals at second tier level for Watford, Derby County and Wolves before moving to Ashton Gate, netted in each of the first three league games of the new 2022/23 season.

BLACKBURN ROVERS
LEWIS TRAVIS

All-action central midfielder Lewis Travis was at the heart of Blackburn Rovers' impressive 2021/22 Championship campaign featuring in all bar one of the club's league games last season.

With the ability to carry the ball forward and help his team turn defence into attack, 25-year-old Travis has won many admirers for his energetic displays in the Rovers engine room.

BURNLEY
JAY RODRIGUEZ

Now in his second spell at Turf Moor, Burnley-born forward Jay Rodriguez is expected to have a big role to play for the Clarets in 2022/23 as the club looks to bounce back to the Premier League at the first attempt.

A former England international, Rodriguez played top-flight football for Southampton and WBA before rejoining the Clarets in 2019.

BLACKPOOL
THEO CORBEANU

Blackpool signed Canadian international forward Theo Corbeanu on a season-long loan from Wolves in July 2022.

Standing at 6ft 3ins, the 20-year-old brings a real presence to the Seasiders' attack and was on target in both of Blackpool's thrilling 3-3 draws against Burnley and Bristol City in August and following the sale of Josh Bowler he could well be the go-to man for goals at Bloomfield Road in 2022/23.

CARDIFF CITY
MAX WATTERS

Exciting striker Max Watters will be looking to cement his place in the Cardiff City attack in 2022/23. After joining the Bluebirds in January 2021 from Crawley, Watters was loaned to League One MK Dons in 2021/22.

However, Cardiff boss Steve Morison has handed Max the chance to make his mark with a series of starts as Cardiff's got the new season underway in impressive form.

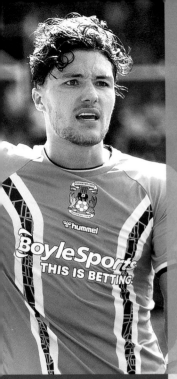

COVENTRY CITY

CALLUM O'HARE

Attacking midfielder Callum O'Hare enjoyed a highly impressive 2021/22 season and has gained the reputation of being both City's star performer and one of the most creative midfielders operating in the Championship.

With fantastic close control and superb awareness of teammates, O'Hare is blessed with great balance when in possession and the eye for a decisive pass.

LUTON TOWN

ELIJAH ADEBAYO

Elijah Adebayo topped the Luton Town scoring charts last season with 16 Championship goals at the Hatters reached the end-of-season Play-Offs.

A strong target man, Adebayo is expected to form an impressive strike partnership at Kenilworth Road this season with Luton new boy Carlton Morris who joined in the summer from Barnsley.

HUDDERSFIELD TOWN

JORDAN RHODES

Striker Jordan Rhodes has netted over 200 career goals since emerging though the Ipswich Town youth system back in 2007.

Now in his second spell with Huddersfield Town, 32-year-old Rhodes scored 87 goals in 148 outings during his first spell at the club. He returned to the Terriers in 2021 and scored the winning goal in last season's Play-Off semi-final against Luton Town.

MIDDLESBROUGH

MATT CROOKS

An all-action attacking midfielder who can also operate as an out-and-out striker, Matt Crooks joined Middlesbrough in the summer of 2021.

Signed on the back of a number of impressive seasons with Rotherham United, Crooks hit double figures in his first season at the Riverside and is sure to play a big part for Chris Wilder's team this time around.

HULL CITY

OSCAR ESTUPINAN

The Tigers completed the signing of Columbian international striker Oscar Estupinan in July 2022.

His arrival created a level of excitement around the MKM Stadium and the Columbian soon showed his capabilities with both goals as Hull pulled off a surprise victory over Norwich City in August 2022. A strong and mobile front man, Estupinan's goals may well help fire the Tigers up the table this season.

MILLWALL

BARTOSZ BIALKOWSKI

Polish international keeper Bartosz Bialkowski has been ever present in the Lions' last two Championship campaigns.

The 6ft 4in stopper is widely regarded as one of the most reliable goalkeepers in the division. Blessed with excellent reflexes, Bialkowski is an intimidating opponent in one-on-one situations and his command of the penalty area certainly provides great confidence for those operating in front of him

NORWICH CITY

TEEMU PUKKI

A Championship title winner on each occasion that he has played at this level, City's Finnish international striker will be searching a hat-trick of promotions from the second tier in 2022/23.

A real threat in and around the penalty area, Pukki netted 29 goals in the Canaries' 2018/19 title-winning campaign and 26 two season later as they went up as champions.

READING

THOMAS INCE

A much-travelled forward, Thomas Ince joined Reading on loan from Stoke City in January 2022 and played a key role him helping the Royals retain their Championship status last season.

Playing under the management of his father, Paul, Ince Jnr then joined Reading on a permanent basis in the summer of 2022. His attacking play and appetite to shoot from distance have won him great popularity with the Reading fans.

ROTHERHAM UNITED

DAN BARLASER

Goalscoring midfielder Dan Barlaser weighed in with nine goals in Rotherham United's League One promotion-winning campaign.

He progressed through the Newcastle United Academy and after gaining valuable experience on loan with the Millers he joined on a permanent basis in October 2020. Seen as the man that makes United tick, a great deal will be expected of the 25-year-old former England youth international in 2022/23.

PRESTON NORTH END

EMIL RIIS JAKOBSEN

Former Denmark U21 international forward Emil Riis Jakobsen enjoyed a highly productive 2021/22 season with Preston North End.

A powerful 6ft 3in frontman, he was the side's standout performer with 20 goals in all competitions last season. The 24-year-old is blessed with great physical strength while also displaying calmness in front of goal.

SHEFFIELD UNITED

OLIVER NORWOOD

Northern Ireland international midfielder Oliver Norwood is something of a Championship promotion-winning specialist.

The 31-year-old has previously won promotion from this division with Brighton, Fulham and as a Sheffield United player in 2018/19. He scored his first goal of the new season as the Blades defeated Blackburn Rovers 3-0 in the opening month of the season.

QUEENS PARK RANGERS

ILIAS CHAIR

The creative spark in the QPR team, Moroccan international Ilias Chair chipped in with nine Championship goals in 2021/22.

A true midfield playmaker, Chair has the ability to open up the tightest of defences and pick out teammates with his exquisite range of passing. The skilful Moroccan is sure to be the man that new Rangers boss Mike Beale looks to build his team around.

STOKE CITY

DWIGHT GAYLE

Much-travelled goal-getter Gayle joined Stoke City from Newcastle United in the summer of 2022.

A nimble front man with the ability to score all manner of goals, his arrival at Stoke was met with great delight. While on loan at WBA in 2018/19 he riffled home an impressive 23 Championship goals and the Potters with be hopeful of a good goal return from their new signing this season.

CHAMPIONSHIP DANGER MEN

24 STARS TO WATCH OUT FOR DURING 2022/23

KEINAN DAVIS

Following an impressive loan spell with Nottingham Forest last season, Aston Villa striker Keinan Davis will be keen to help the Hornets push for an instant return to the Premier League having agreed a season-long loan at Vicarage Road.

Standing at 6ft and 3ins, the 24-year-old striker has pace and power in abundance and is sure to thrill the Watford fans during his loan spell.

SUNDERLAND

ROSS STEWART

On target in SAFC's 2-0 League One Play-Off final victory over Wycombe Wanderers at Wembley, striker Stewart riffled home an impressive 26 goals in all competitions last season.

The Scotland international wasted little time in stepping up to the plate at Championship level as he netted two goals in his first three league games of the new 2022/23 season for the Black Cats.

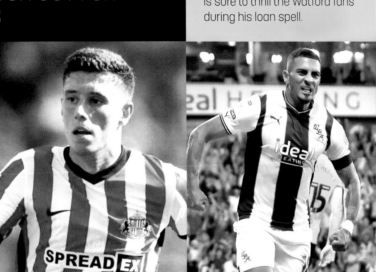

WEST BROMWICH ALBION

KARLAN GRANT

Former Charlton Athletic and Huddersfield Town striker Karlan Grant scored 18 times in West Bromwich's Albion's 2021/22 Championship campaign.

The 25-year-old appears to be the go to man for goals again in 2022/23 for Steve Bruce's men and has already been on target in the Championship and EFL Cup this season.

SWANSEA CITY

MICHAEL OBAFEMI

A two-goal hero in Swansea City's 4-0 thrashing of South Wales rivals Cardiff City last season, pacy striker Michael Obafemi netted twelve Championship goals for the Swans last season.

Having formed a great understanding with fellow front man Joel Piroe in 2021/22, Swans' boss Russell Martin will have great hopes for Republic of Ireland international Obamfemi again in 2022/23.

WIGAN ATHLETIC

CALLUM LANG

A product of the Wigan Athletic academy, Liverpool-born forward Callum Lang has firmly established himself in the Latics' first team as an attacking player with the ability to create chances for team-mates while also score goals himself.

The 23-year-old was in exceptional form throughout 2021/22 when he made 42 League One appearances and scored 15 as the Latics marched to the title.

4
HAMZA
CHOUDHURY

TRUE OR FALSE?

Here are ten fun footy True or False teasers for you to tackle! Good luck...

ANSWERS ON PAGE 62

WATFORD

2. The FIFA World Cup in 2026 is due to be hosted in the USA, Mexico and Canada

3. Manchester City's former ground was called Maine Park

1. England star Harry Kane has only ever played club football for Spurs

4. Liverpool's Jurgen Klopp has never managed the German national team

5. Gareth Southgate succeeded Roy Hodgson as England manager

6. Manchester United's Old Trafford has the largest capacity in the Premier League

7. Jordan Pickford began his career at Everton

8. Huddersfield Town's nickname is the Terriers

9. Watford goalkeeper Ben Hamer was signed from Cardiff City

10. Ismaila Sarr scored five Premier League goals last season

43

STATSports

NUMBER OF SEASONS
WITH THE HORNETS:

14

WATFORD
LEAGUE APPEARANCES:

415

WATFORD LEAGUE GOALS:

148

PLAYER OF THE SEASON WINNER:

Never

LEGEND

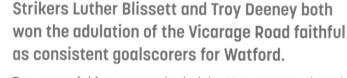

LUTHER BLISSETT

WATFORD ACHIEVEMENTS:

Division Four champions 1977/78
Division Three runners-up 1978/79
Division Two runners-up 1981/82
Division One runners-up 1982/83

MAJOR STRENGTH:

A natural goalscorer who was
a threat to the opposition either
in the air or on the deck

INTERNATIONAL ACTION:

Luther marked his England debut with
a hat-trick against Luxembourg while still
plying his club trade at Vicarage Road

FINEST HOUR:

Blissett topped the Hornets'
scoring charts with 19 First
Division goals in 1982/83

**Strikers Luther Blissett and Troy Deeney both
won the adulation of the Vicarage Road faithful
as consistent goalscorers for Watford.**

Two powerful front men who led the Hornets' attack and
embraced the responsibility of being Watford's go-to men for
goals throughout their Vicarage Road careers. Both players
possessed great physical presence and ensured that any
central defender who was challenged with the task of marking
them would certainly have known they'd been in a game.

Each player boasted an impressive goals-to-games ratio
but who was the best? Well that's for you to decide and here
are a selection of facts and figures from their time with the
Hornets to help you make your choice...

Once again, it's a tough call...!

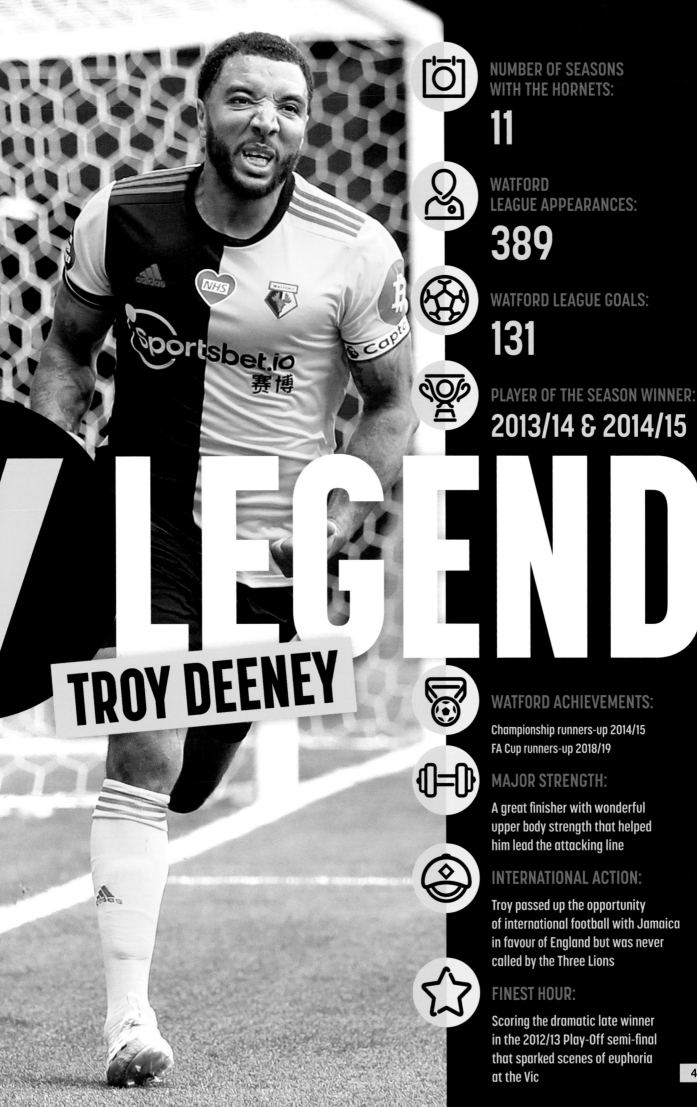

NUMBER OF SEASONS WITH THE HORNETS:

11

WATFORD LEAGUE APPEARANCES:

389

WATFORD LEAGUE GOALS:

131

PLAYER OF THE SEASON WINNER:

2013/14 & 2014/15

LEGEND

TROY DEENEY

WATFORD ACHIEVEMENTS:

Championship runners-up 2014/15
FA Cup runners-up 2018/19

MAJOR STRENGTH:

A great finisher with wonderful
upper body strength that helped
him lead the attacking line

INTERNATIONAL ACTION:

Troy passed up the opportunity
of international football with Jamaica
in favour of England but was never
called by the Three Lions

FINEST HOUR:

Scoring the dramatic late winner
in the 2012/13 Play-Off semi-final
that sparked scenes of euphoria
at the Vic

CLUB SEARCH

EVERY TEAM OF THE CHAMPIONSHIP IS HIDDEN IN THE GRID, EXCEPT FOR ONE... CAN YOU WORK OUT WHICH ONE?

```
J B R A L G V N O R W I C H C I T Y M H
A I M O U Z E K F X R W F U C C D I S W
B R I S T O L C I T Y C B L A E S W P E
L M D A O H V E L P D N A L R E D N U S
A I D C N B E L W L O Q I C D W Y R L T
C N L I T U D R E I A V A I I Q P D O B
K G E T O U N U P U W H T F I T E L R
B H S E W H E B N A I O L Y F M U T S O
U A B L N Y H T V R M J N L C H D I C M
R M R H U O T K L N C U S G I J J N Y W
N C O T M A R I Y O W T N D T M Q U T I
R I U A B U O T C A O I E I Y U R D I C
O T G N U F N S T A D P G M T M X L C H
V Y H A Y S N F C A E I K A S E M E E A
E I G G E G O I E K O S B C S Y D I K L
R A Q I L R T R P L U E N O A O E F O B
S H T W D Z S F O E G T X A D L R F T I
D B U R N L E Y R A S O A K W I B E S O
C O V E N T R Y C I T Y R F N S B H Z N
Q U E E N S P A R K R A N G E R S S A H
```

Birmingham City
Blackburn Rovers
Blackpool
Bristol City
Burnley
Cardiff City

Coventry City
Huddersfield Town
Hull City
Luton Town
Middlesbrough
Millwall

Norwich City
Preston North End
Queens Park Rangers
Reading
Rotherham United
Sheffield United

Stoke City
Sunderland
Swansea City
Watford
West Bromwich Albion
Wigan Athletic

CRAIG
CATHCART
15

WHICH BALL?

Can you work out which is the actual match ball in these two action pics?

48

ANSWERS ON PAGE 62

NAME THE SEASON

Can you recall the campaign when these magic moments occurred? Good luck...

WATFORD

ANSWERS ON PAGE 62

1. In which season did Chelsea last win the UEFA Champions League?

2. When were Manchester United last Premier League champions?

3. At the end of which season were England crowned World Cup winners?

4. In which season did Aleksandar Mitrovic net 43 Championship goals for Fulham?

5. In which season did Leicester City become Premier League champions?

6. When did Tottenham Hotspur last reach the League Cup final?

7. In which season were Sheffield United last promoted to the Premier League?

8. When did Manchester City win their first Premier League title?

9. During which season did Troy Deeney make his Watford debut?

10. In which season did Watford defeat Leeds United in the Championship Play-Off final?

49

Stake.com

Watford Women

Watford Women's recent seasons have provided a rollercoaster of emotions for players, coaching staff and supporters, with big wins, frustrating moments, triumph and defeat taking place in a short space of time.

The Golden Girls, then known as Watford Ladies, enjoyed four years in the second league of women's football between 2014 and 2018, in their first seasons under the Watford FC name.

Moving into the Women's National League ahead of the 2018/19 season, the Hornets achieved a respectable fifth-place finish in their first campaign in the third tier, playing at Kings Langley FC's Orbital Fasteners Stadium. Led by hometown hero Helen Ward, Watford began to build a side capable of promotion back to the second division.

Sitting second with three games in hand on first-placed Crawley Wasps, the National League season was curtailed in 2019/20 due to the Coronavirus outbreak, and further lockdowns suspended the 2020/21 season also, with the Hornets in top spot. Between the two seasons, Watford Ladies became Watford Women to represent the change in societal language.

Ahead of the 2021/22 season, the club were awarded promotion via upward movement, securing a place in the FA Women's Championship. Although Watford were unable to avoid relegation in that campaign, their aim is to immediately return to where they belong under Head Coach Damon Lathrope, now playing their games at Wealdstone's Grosvenor Vale in the FA Women's National League South.

1. WHO AM I?

2. WHO AM I?

4. WHO AM I?

3. WHO AM I?

ANSWERS ON PAGE 62

WHO ARE YER?

Can you figure out who each of these Hornets stars is?

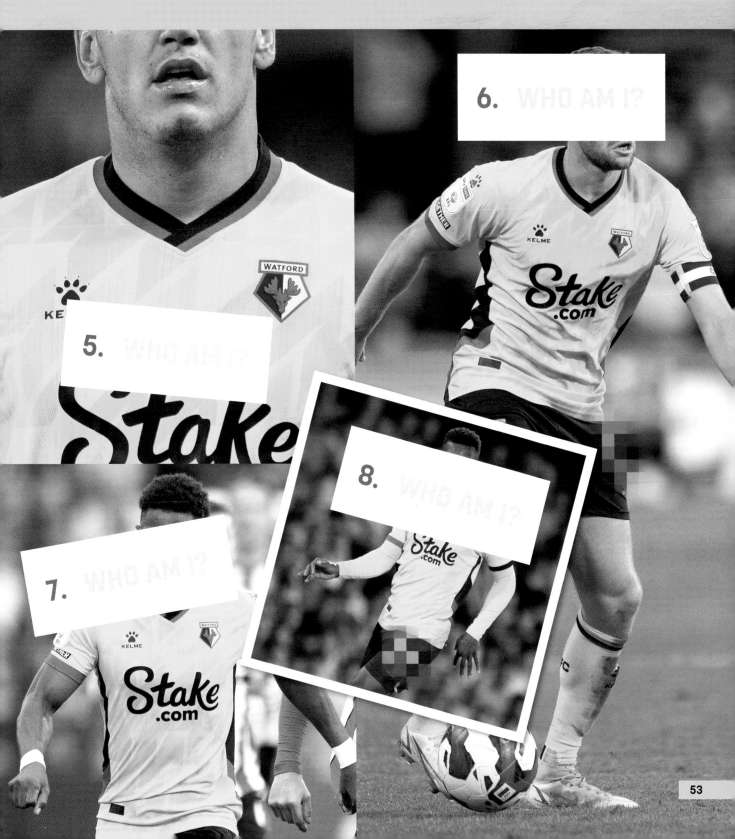

5. WHO AM I?

6. WHO AM I?

7. WHO AM I?

8. WHO AM I?

JOÃO
PEDRO
10

Can you colour
in this picture
of João Pedro?

TRUE
COLOURS

PREMIER LEAGUE CHAMPIONS
Liverpool

CHAMPIONSHIP WINNERS
Watford

FAST FORWARD>>

Do your predictions for 2022/23 match our own?...

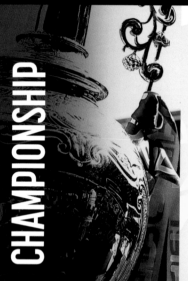

CHAMPIONSHIP

CHAMPIONSHIP RUNNERS-UP
Norwich City

PREMIER LEAGUE

PREMIER LEAGUE RUNNERS-UP
Chelsea

PREMIER LEAGUE TOP SCORER
Erling Haaland

CHAMPIONSHIP TOP SCORER
João Pedro

LEAGUE ONE TOP SCORER
Conor Chaplin

FA CUP

FA CUP WINNERS
Spurs

LEAGUE CUP WINNERS
Leicester City

LEAGUE CUP

LEAGUE ONE CHAMPIONS
Derby County

CHAMPIONS LEAGUE

CHAMPIONS LEAGUE WINNERS
Real Madrid

LEAGUE ONE RUNNERS-UP
Oxford United

LEAGUE ONE

EUROPA LEAGUE WINNERS
Roma

EUROPA LEAGUE

57

NUMBER OF SEASONS WITH THE HORNETS:

2

WATFORD LEAGUE APPEARANCES:

89

PLAYER OF THE SEASON WINNER:

1990/91

LEGEND

DAVID JAMES

WATFORD ACHIEVEMENTS:

No promotions were achieved or finals reached during David's Watford career

MAJOR STRENGTH:

A big penalty-box presence who was always happy to take command of his area

INTERNATIONAL ACTION:

David was capped by England at U21 level while with the Hornets

FINEST HOUR:

An impressive ever-present 1990/91 campaign as Watford escaped the threat of relegation

Watford Football Club has a long and proud history of fielding excellent goalkeepers and both David James and Ben Foster have starred in between the posts for the Hornets.

As the last line of defence, both James and Foster produced a host of match-winning saves throughout their Vicarage Road careers while marshalling the defensive unit in front of them. While Foster proved to be an inspired loan signing and later a permanent arrival, James of course progressed through the youth ranks. But who was the best? It's a tricky one to decide and here are a number of facts and figures from their time at the Vic to help you reach your decision...

Yet again, it's certainly a tough call...!

NUMBER OF SEASONS WITH THE HORNETS:

6

WATFORD LEAGUE APPEARANCES:

198

PLAYER OF THE SEASON WINNER:

2006/07

LEGEND

BEN FOSTER

WATFORD ACHIEVEMENTS:

Championship Play-Off winners 2005/06
FA Cup runners-up 2018/19
Championship promotion 2020/21

MAJOR STRENGTH:

An athletic 'keeper with great reflexes and superb anticipation of danger

INTERNATIONAL ACTION:

Ben made his England debut during his second loan spell with the Hornets

FINEST HOUR:

A Play-Off final clean sheet as Watford defeated Leeds United to secure promotion to the Premier League in 2005/06

IDENTIFY THE STAR

Can you put a name to the football stars in these ten teasers?

Good luck...

ANSWERS ON PAGE 62

1. Manchester City's title-winning 'keeper Ederson shared the 2021/22 Golden Glove award for the number of clean sheets with which Premier League rival?

2. Which Portuguese superstar re-joined Manchester United in the 2021/22 season?

3. Can you name the Brazilian forward who joined Aston Villa in May 2022 following a loan spell at Villa Park?

4. Who became Arsenal manager in 2019?

5. Who scored the winning goal in the 2021/22 UEFA Champions League final?

6. After 550 games for West Ham United, which long-serving midfielder announced his retirement in 2022?

7. Who took the mantle of scoring Brentford's first Premier League goal?

8. Who scored the final goal for Manchester City in their 2021/22 Premier League title-winning season?

9. Which player topped the Hornets scoring charts in 2021/22?

10. Who joined Watford from Charleroi in July 2022?

KEN

SEMA

12

ANSWERS

PAGE 26 · MULTIPLE CHOICE

1. C. 2. B. 3. A. 4. B. 5. C. 6. A. 7. B. 8. B. 9. B. 10. C.

PAGE 28 · FAN'TASTIC

PAGE 43 · TRUE OR FALSE?

1. False, Harry played on loan for Leyton Orient, Millwall, Norwich City & Leicester City. 2. True. 3. False, it was called Maine Road.
4. True. 5. False, Gareth succeeded Sam Allardyce. 6. True.
7. False, Jordan began his career at Sunderland. 8. True.
9. False, he was signed from Swansea City. 10. True.

PAGE 46 · CLUB SEARCH

Huddersfield Town

PAGE 48 · WHICH BALL?

PAGE 49 · NAME THE SEASON

1. 2020/21. 2. 2012/13. 3. 1965/66. 4. 2021/22. 5. 2015/16.
6. 2020/21. 7. 2018/19. 8. 2011/12. 9. 2010/11. 10. 2005/06.

PAGE 52 · WHO ARE YER?

1. Edo Kayembe. 2. Craig Cathcart. 3. Joao Pedro.
4. Francisco Sierralta. 5. Rey Manaj. 6. Tom Cleverley.
7. Emmanuel Dennis. 8. Christian Kabasele.

PAGE 60 · IDENTIFY THE STAR

1. Allison Becker. 2. Cristiano Ronaldo. 3. Philippe Coutinho.
4. Mikel Arteta. 5. Vinicius Junior. 6. Mark Noble.
7. Sergi Canos. 8. Ilkay Gundogan. 9. Emmanuel Dennis.
          10. Vakoun Issouf Bayo.